IMAGES OF

MW00534685

SS POLIZEI AT WAR 1940–1945

A HISTORY OF THE DIVISION

RARE PHOTOGRAPHS FROM WARTIME ARCHIVES

Ian Baxter

Pen & Sword
MILITARY

First published in Great Britain in 2018 by
PEN & SWORD MILITARY
An imprint of
Pen & Sword Books Ltd
47 Church Street
Barnsley
South Yorkshire
S70 2AS

Copyright © Ian Baxter, 2018

ISBN 978-1-47389-097-8

The right of Ian Baxter to be identified as author of this work has been asserted by him in accordance with the Copyright, Designs and Patents Act 1988.

A CIP catalogue record for this book is available from the British Library.

All rights reserved. No part of this book may be reproduced or transmitted in any form or by any means, electronic or mechanical including photocopying, recording or by any information storage and retrieval system, without permission from the Publisher in writing.

Typeset by Concept, Huddersfield, West Yorkshire HD4 5JL.
Printed and bound in England by CPI Group (UK) Ltd, Croydon CR0 4YY.

Pen & Sword Books Limited incorporates the imprints of Atlas, Archaeology, Aviation, Discovery, Family History, Fiction, History, Maritime, Military, Military Classics, Politics, Select, Transport, True Crime, Air World, Frontline Publishing, Leo Cooper, Remember When, Seaforth Publishing, The Praetorian Press, Wharncliffe Local History, Wharncliffe Transport, Wharncliffe True Crime and White Owl.

For a complete list of Pen & Sword titles please contact
PEN & SWORD BOOKS LIMITED
47 Church Street, Barnsley, South Yorkshire S70 2AS, England
E-mail: enquiries@pen-and-sword.co.uk
Website: www.pen-and-sword.co.uk

Contents

About the Author

Ian Baxter is a military historian who specialises in German twentieth century military history. He has written more than fifty books including *Poland – The Eighteen Day Victory March*, *Panzers In North Africa*, *The Ardennes Offensive*, *The Western Campaign*, *The 12th SS Panzer-Division Hitlerjugend*, *The Waffen-SS on the Western Front*, *The Waffen-SS on the Eastern Front*, *The Red Army at Stalingrad*, *Elite German Forces of World War II*, *Armoured Warfare*, *German Tanks of War*, *Blitzkrieg*, *Panzer-Divisions at War*, *Hitler's Panzers*, *German Armoured Vehicles of World War Two*, *Last Two Years of the Waffen-SS at War*, *German Soldier Uniforms and Insignia*, *German Guns of the Third Reich*, *Defeat to Retreat: The Last Years of the German Army At War 1943-45*, *Operation Bagration – the Destruction of Army Group Centre*, *German Guns of the Third Reich*, *Rommel and the Afrika Korps*, *U-Boat War*, and most recently *The Sixth Army and the Road to Stalingrad*. He has written over a hundred articles including 'Last days of Hitler', 'Wolf's Lair', 'The Story of the V1 and V2 Rocket Programme', 'Secret Aircraft of World War Two', 'Rommel at Tobruk', 'Hitler's War With his Generals', 'Secret British Plans to Assassinate Hitler', 'The SS at Arnhem', 'Hitlerjugend', 'Battle of Caen 1944', 'Gebirgsjäger at War', 'Panzer Crews', 'Hitlerjugend Guerrillas', 'Last Battles in the East', 'The Battle of Berlin', and many more. He has also reviewed numerous military studies for publication, supplied thousands of photographs and important documents to various publishers and film production companies worldwide, and lectures to various schools, colleges and universities throughout the United Kingdom and the Republic of Ireland.

Introduction

Formed in 1939, the Polizei Division were not considered initially an SS fighting force, and this status was reflected in the quality of the equipment they were issued. Following operations in France and then Russia, it was not until 1942 that the division was transferred to the Waffen-SS, and eventually upgraded to a Panzergrenadier division – the 4th SS-Polizei-Panzergrenadier Division.

Using rare and unpublished photographs accompanied by captions and text, this book describes the history of the division, its fighting tactics, the uniforms and the battles it fought alongside Wehrmacht and other SS fighting units. It describes how this police unit evolved, how it marched and battled its way across the Low Countries, then the Eastern Front, and then, in its last year, where it fought in the Balkans and Greece (where it committed one of the worst atrocities of the war). It shows how it was forced to withdraw under overwhelming enemy superiority and, much depleted, was moved to Pomerania where it continued resisting fanatically. In the war's last days it fought to defend Berlin where many soldiers fought to the death.

This book is a unique glimpse into one of the most famous fighting machines of the Second World War and a great addition to the library of any reader interested in Waffen-SS history.

Chapter One

Origins

Even before the Germans attacked Poland in September 1939, Himmler wanted to create a third division that was not technically SS, unlike the LSSAH, SS-VT units (later Das Reich) and unofficially the Totenkopfverbände (Death's Head). This new division would be formed from ordinary policemen, or Ordnungspolizei. From its conception it was planned to be part of the military arm of Himmler's growing empire which would be capable of fighting alongside both Wehrmacht and SS-VT troops and still police the local area with force. The Polizei division, although not titled as a division at that time, was created at the end of the Polish campaign in early October 1939. Some 15,000 members of the Ordnungspolizei were drafted into units of the artillery and signals units that were transferred from the Wehrmacht. During its creation these men were not recruited as SS troops, but as policemen and wearing regular army uniforms.

Generalleutnant der Polizei Karl Pfeffer-Wildenbruch was appointed the Polizei's first commander, and with it was also commissioned as an SS-Gruppenführer. His task was to equip and train the police unit to become a fully-fledged fighting machine. However, it was poorly funded, with resources going to the new SS units like the LSSAH and SS-VT. It was a poor-grade unit and lacked the physical and ideological qualities of the original armed SS formations. There was also resentment within the ranks, as many of the men were middle-aged and had not wanted to be taken away from their chosen professions as policemen to act as soldiers. Nonetheless, they began its training in the Black Forest and was sent on internal security duties in Poland.

The new recruits, although not yet imbued with the same enthusiasm as their SS counterparts, still trained and undertook their service in relatively good spirits. Wearing their field grey uniforms, bearing police instead of the SS insignia, the men trained with equipment that mainly consisted of captured Czech weapons.

Military training was often laborious for the trainers as many of the recruits had no combat experience or military knowledge. Some also proved to be 'gun shy', or simply had no aptitude, despite patient encouragement. However, once familiar with their weapons they were taught infantry assault techniques, with emphasis on ferocity and speed in attack. The recruits soon learnt this was key to obtaining an enemy position quickly and efficiently and minimising casualties.

Ideologically, the teachings in the Polizei were kept to a minimum. It was unlike that of the SS order where trainers reinforced each recruit with Germanic virtues, producing men who believed in their destiny as missionaries of a new Aryan order to rule the world with an iron fist. Here in the ranks of the Polizei, the men were taught to fight and stay alive. They were told that they were fighting to make their country strong and fulfilling their personal oath to their Führer.

During the first part of 1940, the SS continued to expand. In March, the SST-VT officially became the Waffen-SS (Weapon-SS), comprising the reinforced LSSAH (Leibstandarte SS Adolf Hitler), now at regimental strength, the newly formed SS Totenkopf Division, and the Polizei Division. The SS-VT had been formed during the closing days of the Polish campaign by amalgamating the three SS-VT *truppen* together as Deutschland, Germania and Der Führer. This formation would later become the infamous Das Reich division, and take centre stage replacing the Polizei division as the third SS division in the Waffen-SS. Polizei would become the fourth.

The men of the Leibstandarte would continue to receive nothing but the best equipment and hardware, while the Polizei, which was not really expected to take an active role in future fighting, would make do being supplied with obsolescent horse-drawn weapons. The Polizei were not even given priority over the regular Heer. Equipment for the formation was often extremely slow to come through, and wrangling over the distribution of weapons was a constant problem.

Even as preparations were made for war against the West, there were already acute shortages of guns due to the drastic expansion of the Wehrmacht and their need to be ready for action. If the SS divisions were to function properly they needed their own integral artillery battalions. Moreover, these units needed to be motorized and would require large numbers of vehicles to tow guns and move troops quickly to forward areas of the battlefield.

In spite of shortages, the SS were to take part in operations against the West. Both the Leibstandarte and SS-VT were already bloodied from Poland, and were thus suited for front-line tasks. However, the Totenkopf and the Polizei divisions were untried in battle, and consequently did not inspire confidence in the Heer units who would have to fight alongside them. Both divisions were ordered into reserve and were to play initially no active role in the campaign.

(**Opposite, above**) A Polizei officer gives out his orders during a training exercise. Although formed under the authority of Reichsführer Heinrich Himmler, the Polizei was not technically SS at this early period of the war. Prevented by the army from recruiting soldiers from the general population, Himmler did however have a source of manpower in the police, which he controlled, and the division was made up from members of the Ordnungspolizei, the Police force.

(**Opposite, below**) Two 10.5cm howitzer crew members prepare to hitch the gun to its limber during a training exercise. Note their gas mask canisters slung around to their front so they can easily sit in the limber.

(**Above**) A photograph taken of a 10.5cm howitzer at a training barracks in 1939. Note on the left sleeve of the soldier straddling the cannon is the infamous SS eagle. In the foreground the man on the left is an NCO and is identifiable by the braid loop at the base of his shoulder straps.

(**Opposite, above**) A second photograph taken at the same training barracks of a 10.5cm howitzer.

(**Opposite, below**) What appears to be a photograph of a complete artillery Abteilung lined up during a training exercise. In the foreground is a caisson attached to a limber. The guns are the 7.5cm FK16 nA.

A candidate wearing a white denim work uniform during a training exercise, armed with the MG34 machine gun on a bipod. Each artillery battery was assigned two MG34 machine squads to protect its position against both aerial and ground attack.

An artillery regiment with their pristine looking 10.5cm howitzer at their training barracks during what appears to be a ceremonial occasion.

Two photographs taken in sequence showing SS-Artillerie-Regiment 4 during manoeuvres in the early spring of 1940. Wearing their white training garments these artillerymen are put through their paces simulating on-the-march towing their artillery and equipment. Even in 1940 the German army's main mode of transport was still animal draught.

(**Opposite, above**) What appears to be some kind of ceremony at a training camp in 1940 complete with military band and 10.5cm le.FH 18 light field howitzer. Generally all German infantry divisions had organic field artillery regiments. These comprised batteries that contained the 10.5cm, which was the most popular artillery piece in the German arsenal during the early war period.

(**Opposite, below**) Polizei troops belonging to an SS-Artillerie-Regiment during a parade ceremony in early 1940. Two 10.5cm le.FH 18 light field howitzers are placed at right angles with a group of stacked Karabiner 98K bolt-action rifles positioned between them. The 10.5cm was the standard field howitzer used by both the Polizei, SS, and regular army during this early war period.

(**Above**) Two Polizei troops are seen during a training exercise. One nearest the photographer is armed with the standard German Karabiner 98K bolt-action rifle, while his troop leader is armed with the MP38/40. Instead of SS equipment the Polizei were often equipped with old and captured hardware. The troops too where considerably older than other SS men, and they lacked poor training.

Two photographs taken in sequence on manoeuvres during the early winter of 1940; men of SS-Artillerie-Regiment 4 are seen in the snow. Clad in the standard army great coat wearing head scarf and Wehrmacht M1938 field caps, but displaying the early style front metal cap skull button and branch-coloured soutache, they stand next to their 10.5cm le.FH18 light field howitzer with a horse.

A close-up of the 10.5cm le.FH18 light field howitzer in the snow during early 1940, complete with unattached caisson. The gun weighed nearly two tons and fired a 14.4kg shell to a maximum range of 10,675 metres. Note the letter 'D' painted in white on the inside of the gun shield. This denoted that the gun was the fourth in the battery.

Chapter Two

Western Front (1940)

For the attack against the west the German Army was divided into three groups – Army Groups A, B and C. The main strike would be given to Army Group A, which would drive its armoured units through the Ardennes, then swing round across the plains of northern France and then make straight for the Channel coast, thereby cutting the Allied force in half. The main enemy concentration in Belgium would be assaulted by Army Group A advancing from the south and Army Group B from the north. The task of Army Group B was to occupy Holland with motorized forces and to prevent the linking up of the Dutch army with the Anglo-Belgian force. It was to destroy the Belgian frontier defences by a rapid and powerful attack and throw the enemy back over the line between Antwerp and Namur.

Army Group C, which was the most southern of the three army groups, was to engage the garrison of the Maginot Line, penetrating it if possible.

Distributed between the three army groups, the Germans deployed twenty-nine divisions under Army Group B in the north and forty-four divisions under Army Group A in the centre. Army Group C, with seventeen divisions, covered the southern flank and threatened the French position on its eastern flank.

Taking part in the attack were the Leibstandarte and SS-VT divisions assembled for action in Army Group B. Totenkopf formed part of the reserves available to Army Group A, while the Polizei Division was assigned to Army Group C, positioned opposite the Maginot Line. Here Polizei units tended to their horses and equipment and waited with no prospect of attacking alongside the SS or other Heer formations.

By the end of the first day of the attack in the west, Belgian resistance had been overwhelmed and the cavalry of the French 9th Army brushed aside. Although the French 7th Army had reached Breda on 11 May, by the next day it was in retreat under strong pressure from General Heinz Guderian's Panzers. By the evening of that same day, the Panzer units reached the Meuse along a 100-mile front, from Sedan to Dinant. They had advanced nearly ninety miles in three days. As the whole front began to crumble in indecision and confusion, the demoralized French Army tended to its wounds and withdrew to Antwerp along roads clogged with refugees.

By 15 May, the Dutch army formally surrendered, although isolated units continued to fight a grim defensive battle until 17 May. As German troops occupied Holland with lightning speed, Belgium's capital capitulated. By 18 May the 5th Panzer Division reported that it had reached the northern bank of the Sambre. Two days later, the first Panzers came in sight of the Channel coast. In no more than eleven days, the Germans had advanced 400 miles and done what the German army had failed to accomplish in four years during the First World War.

Over the next couple of weeks the Wehrmacht, together with their SS counterparts, drove deeper into France capturing more villages and towns. On 9 June the Polizei division was finally released from reserve and for the first time in its brief existence moved to its staging point and was ordered to advance with animal draught across the Aisen River and the Ardennes Canal. Wearing their distinctive grey army uniforms with Polizei insignia, the men marched forward into battle, many now equipped with the standard German Karabiner 98K bolt-action rifle slung over their shoulders. It was not long before these units were embroiled in the fray, and launched a number of attacks in the Argonne Forest, where it came into contact with French forces that were defending frantically with their rearguard. Here the Polizei tried bitterly to contest every foot of ground, and at times it seemed they would be overwhelmed by French firepower. It was not until after bloody hand-to-hand fighting that the Polizei managed to break through the lines and overcame their foe.

By the time the cease-fire came on 22 June, the Polizei was once again withdrawn from operational duties and put in reserve. The performance of the division had been mixed. While they lacked weapons and proper equipment, the troops had not been aggressive and fanatical enough. In spite an unconvincing start, its commanders were determined to improve its reputation on the battlefield.

Following the defeat of France, the division remained in the country in reserve. Here it strengthened its formation with additional troops and equipment, but it still fell short of what was required. Over the next days and weeks the Polizei Division trained with its artillery for a proposed invasion of Great Britain, which soon lost momentum. Instead, plans were already being drafted for the conquest of the Soviet Union, and for this titanic invasion all available resources and manpower would be drafted to the East, including the Waffen-SS and Polizei.

(**Opposite, above**) A Polizei supply wagon crosses a ditch that has already seen some heavy traffic during operations on the Western Front in June 1940. To prevent vehicles from sinking in boggy terrain, pioneers have laid logs down to allow traffic to pass over them with relative ease. Because Polizei was not motorised and relied mainly on animal draught, the troops found that advancing through forests and across fields was sometimes challenging. Freak downpours could often hinder movement that the division replied on for supplies.

(**Opposite, below**) A group of Polizei officers confer with one of the division's SS photographers in June 1940. Although photographers were an important conduit for transmitting news to the German populace via the Propaganda Ministry in Berlin, many of them were given strict orders not to reveal their men undergoing mundane duties, but only to show the SS in action, and portray them in the most heroic light.

(**Opposite, above**) Polizei *truppen* in a French town during the division's brief advance. The Polizei was primarily a horse-drawn formation, but due to its limited operations in the west this did not seriously curtail its advance. Most of these soldiers have been marching over considerable distances alongside plodding horses. The men were absolutely dependent on animal draught due to the serious lack of vehicles in the division.

(**Above**) Soldiers during a respite in the advance inside a bombed French town in June 1940. Most of the troops are still holding their Kar 98K bolt-action rifles, which suggests the area is either not safe or the stay is temporary. Among sub-machine guns, or machine pistols, as the SS knew them, the MP38/40 was not extensively used by this division until it fought in Russia. However, it did receive small batches of earlier models like the Bergmann MP28.

Two photographs showing bicycle units. On the original caption the image reads, 'Totenkopf und Polizei Westfeldzug 1940'. However, that was incorrect as both these divisions did not advance together in France. The men on bicycle are Polziei.

Polizei on the march along a road in France. For ease of carriage most have shouldered their rifles. The division's first taste of combat came late, when it was employed in assault crossings of the River Aisne at the Ardennes Canal. Once its objectives were secured in this area the division moved onto the Argonne Forest where it fought to capture Les Islettes.

(**Opposite, above**) A Polizei supply convoy on the march along a dusty road in France in June 1940. A supply wagon can be seen being pulled by horses while troops mounted on bicycles are following closely behind.

(**Opposite, below**) Troops belonging to Polizei during a respite inside a ruined French town. It had not been until 9/10 June 1940 that the Polizei was finally permitted to engage in an offensive operation of its own. This photograph was taken a few miles from the Ardennes Canal and it was here that it became heavily embroiled against determined French units.

(**Above**) An interesting photograph showing SS-Artillerie-Regiment 4 halted with horses towing the regiment's caisson during its march in France. Divisional artillery supported the combat troops before and during action, and it was of paramount importance that the division's artillery regiment were powerful as well as manoeuvrable.

(**Opposite, above**) The regiment's commanding officer can be seen leading his men on horseback through a French town. These men more than likely are from SS-Artillerie-Regiment 4. In the distance are supply wagons and what appears to be animals towing caissons.

(**Above**) With their horses and caisson, two Polizei artillerymen pose for the camera during a brief respite in their march through France. A German caisson was a two-wheeled cart designed to carry artillery ammunition and its crew. Limbers and caissons were in great need in the Polizei, especially until 1943.

(**Opposite, below**) Polizei troops stand around a small HF12 small field kitchen wagon (Feldküchenwagen). These field kitchens provided the troops with soups, stews and coffee. The limber carried cooking utensils and equipment.

Two photographs taken in sequence showing the Polizei on the march following a caisson through a French town. The column comprises a number of caissons and limbers all drawn by horse. The men are wearing the standard army greatcoat. This standard pattern greatcoat with its dark blue-green collar can be seen worn without personal equipment.

Troops of the Polizei encamped near the town of Les Islettes. This photograph was taken just before the division was pulled out of the line into reserve on 21 June. Note the Zeltbahn camouflaged tents and the temporary medical field tent. By the look of the shirtless soldiers it was very warm and three of the men bask in the sun playing a gramophone.

Photographed from a limber three Polizei soldiers can be seen wearing the MP38 field cap and M35 greatcoat. The M35 greatcoat was the most common winter garment issued to the troops in the field. It was double-breasted made of high quality woolen-content cloth, the colour a greenish shade of field grey.

(**Above**) Polizei on the march along a road approaching a French town. The troops have all been issued with the standard Wehrmacht M36 field blouse with its typical dark-green facing collars and basic field grey cloth trousers tucked into the M39 short shaft leather marching boots. The men have been issued with the usual rifleman's equipment and weapons: the enlisted-man's leather belt, M1939 infantry leather support straps, two rifle ammunition pouches, small entrenching tool, and S84/98 bayonet with leather frog. Their personal kit was standard comprising M1931 bread bag, M1931 field flask with drinking cup, M31 mess kit, M31 Zeltbahn shelter quarter, and gasmask in its M1938 metal canister. Their weapons comprise two M1924 stick grenades and the standard Karabiner 98K rifle.

(**Opposite, above**) A10.5cm le.FH 18 positioned along a road inside a French town during the initial stages of an opening attack. The cameraman has taken decisive action and takes cover just before the gun is readied for action.

(**Opposite, below**) A battery of 10.5cm le.FH 18s in France. Wherever possible, it was best to conceal artillery at the edge of a tree line, as in this photograph. Note to the right of the photograph an artilleryman holding up an aiming stake. The aiming stake would be set up some distance forward from the gun to serve as a reference point from which to set the gun's deflection.

(**Opposite, above**) Artillerymen pose for the camera onboard a horse-drawn 10.5cm howitzer with caisson along a road. The crewmen often rode on the caisson, but sometimes were compelled to follow on foot to reduce the weight, especially over rough ground.

(**Above**) The Polizei crossing the Ardennes Canal. Bicycles were surprisingly useful, although impeded over difficult terrain. In France the countryside was often flat and good for bicycles.

(**Opposite, below**) The Polizei crossing the Ardennes Canal. Note all the gear and equipment attached to their bicycles. They are all armed with the Kar 98K bolt-action rifle, or Mauser as it was called by the troops.

Two photographs taken in sequence, showing part of a horse-drawn artillery Abteilung on the march advancing along a road. All the crew are wearing the standard Wehrmacht issue M31 Zeltbahn shelter quarter over their service uniform to protect them from the rain. An average artillery regiment in the early war period was authorized with some 2,500 troops and 2,274 horses, the latter of which drew over 200 wagons and artillery caissons.

A 10.5cm battery out in the field. The crew are all wearing the standard Wehrmacht issue M31 Zeltbahn shelter quarter. The battery have purposely separated their weapons at intervals not only for better positioning on the battlefield against ground targets, but to minimize damage from aerial or ground attack.

From the same battery, the a 10.5cm howitzer in the field that has just been unlimbered and is being prepared for a fire mission. Note the tarpaulin that has been draped over the wheels. This was done to afford some camouflage protection by breaking up the shape of the gun.

Two photographs taken in sequence showing the crew of a 10.5cm howitzer posing for the camera during a lull in a fire mission. It was primarily the artillery regiments that were given the task of destroying enemy positions and fortified defences and of conducting counter-battery fire prior to an armoured or infantry assault. Note the covered aluminum buckets used by the crew for unused propellant charges. Gunners preferred aluminum to steel to prevent a spark igniting the charges.

Wearing their M35 greatcoat in the rain, three artillery crewmen can be seen with shells belonging to a 10.5cm le.FH 18 light field howitzer. They are clearly priming the 14.4kg shells for a fire mission.

A 10.5cm howitzer crew located in a muddy field prepare to open fire on a rainy day. The young crewman has primed the shell and is loading the charge into the breech.

Another photograph showing a 10.5cm howitzer crew preparing their weapon for a fire mission in the rain. Note the wicker cases and the primed shells lying on top ready to be fired.

Two photographs taken in sequence showing Polizei preparing the 10.5cm howitzer for a fire mission, and two artillerymen can be seen holding the aiming stake. Apart from tarpaulin draped over the steel wheels, some earth has been piled around the front of the weapon to distort the gun's appearance and alter its distinctive shape.

Photographed in action and this 10.5cm howitzer has just recoiled after firing at a target; the smoke residue can clearly be seen. Note the rammer behind the weapon preparing for another fire mission. Of noticeable interest, purposely laid out in the field is the crew's 98K bolt-action rifles, prepared in case they come under attack.

Two photographs taken in sequence showing artillery crew preparing its position for a fire mission. More than 5,000 of these light 10.5cm field howitzers entered service when the war broke out in 1939, and remained the standard light divisional howitzer throughout the war.

Two photographs taken in sequence showing an artillery crew preparing their 10.5cm howitzer for a fire mission in a soggy field. The crew are all wearing their waterproof Zeltbahnen to help keep them dry. Although these howitzers provided armour-piercing and shaped-charge anti-tank rounds, they were far from being effective anti-tank weapons.

(**Above**) Halted on a road somewhere in France is part of a horse-drawn artillery Abteilung towing 10.5cm howitzers to the battlefront. The 10.5cm howitzer had a good reputation as a reliable and stable weapon that was easy to manoeuvre and use. The carriage had a split trail pattern with folding spades, and had either pressed metal or wood-spoked wheels.

(**Opposite, above**) Halted along a road inside a French town and Polizei artillerymen can be seen standing with their horses, artillery limbers and caissons. Combat experience showed that artillery support was a decisive factor in both defensive and offensive roles. The three light artillery battalions each had three four-gun batteries with 10.5cm howitzers.

(**Opposite, below**) This photograph was taken on 18 June 1940 and shows men of the Polizei resting in a field awaiting further deployment. On that day German forces had captured Rennes, while the 5th Panzer Division had reached Brest.

(**Above**) In a field is a heavy MG34 machine gun squad. The MG34 is mounted on a sustained fire mount. In every artillery battalion there fielded MG34 heavy machine gunners on sustained fire mount, which in 1940 was regarded as more than enough to keep open the flanks for attacking infantry and protect artillery positions.

(**Opposite, above**) Here members of the SS-Polizei-Regiment 4, a security formation, can be seen lining the Avenue Foch as a military band can just be seen passing round to the Arc de Triomphe during the victory parade in Paris on 14 June 1940. This unit was a garrison security force stationed in the French capital and was under the operational command of the Higher SS and Police Leader 'Frankreich'.

(**Opposite, below**) Polizei troops wait while their comrades dig a grave for some of their war dead. When there were many burials to be carried out larger mass graves were often dug. The corpses of the soldiers were then individually laid to rest, alongside each other. Earth was then used to cover the bodies before a cross or SS rune was placed next to where each of the dead soldiers had been laid.

(**Opposite, above**) The grave of a 26-year-old soldier called Karl Koch who was attached to 8th Polizei Rifle Regiment 1 of the Polizei Division. He was killed in France on 10 June 1940. The Polizei suffered particularly heavy casualties in France because of its poorer-quality soldiery and lack of equipment. During its brief deployment on the Western Front, units often found advances to be hard going, as they fought a series of hand-to-hand battles to overcome isolated French units who were putting up stiff opposition.

(**Above**) A grave of two fallen Polizei troops. SS runes have been whitewashed into the freshly dug earth. This type of burial was common, especially for officers and NCOs.

Chapter Three

Holding the Line
(1941)

In January 1941, the Polizei division was put under the control of the SS operations office or the SS-Führungshauptamt, which was responsible for the operational and administrative control of the Waffen-SS, including recruiting and managing special personnel requirements. However, this did not make them members of the SS.

In June the division was transported from France to Army Group North in East Prussia. At this stage Polizei had a divisional strength of 17,347 men. Combat-ready, the division remained in reserve while German forces began concentrating in the east, ready for their part in the attack against Russia.

For the invasion of Russia, code-named Operation Barbarossa, the Wehrmacht assembled some three million men, divided into 105 infantry divisions and 32 Panzer divisions. This was distributed over three Army Groups:

- Army Group North – commanded by General Wilhelm Ritter von Leeb, who had assembled his forces in East Prussia on the Lithuanian frontier. His force provided the main spearhead for the advance on Leningrad.
- Army Group Centre – commanded by General Fedor von Bock, assembled on the 1939 Polish/Russian frontier, both north and south of Warsaw. Bock's force consisted of 42 Infantry Divisions of the 4th and 9th Armies, and Panzer Groups II and III. This was the largest of the three groups.
- Army Group South – commanded by General Gerd von Rundstedt. This was deployed down the longest stretch of border with Russia.

The front reached from central Poland to the Black Sea and was held by one Panzer Group, three German armies, two Rumanian armies, and a Hungarian motorised corps under German command.

Finally, on 22 June, the Eastern Front erupted as the German Army attacked. Army Group North drove its forces at tremendous speed across the Baltic region. General Leeb's force, consisting of 16th and 18th armies, smashed through the Soviet defences. Russian soldiers stood helpless in its path, too shocked to take action. Over the weeks to come, Army Group North continued to smash through enemy positions heading through Lithuania, Latvia and Estonia, towards their objective – Leningrad.

By mid-July Army Group North had broken through south of Pskov and rolled towards Luga. At the rate they were advancing, they would need no more than ten days to reach the outskirts of Leningrad. However, following it success, the Wehrmacht was losing momentum. Not only were supply lines being overstretched, but enemy resistance began to stiffen. In a desperate attempt to blunt the German advance and prevent them from reaching the imperial city, brigades of Russian marines, naval units, and more than 80,000 men from the Baltic Fleet were hastily sent into action against von Leeb. These Russian soldiers were now the sole barrier between Leningrad and the Germans. Although the advance was hampered by increasing enemy resistance, by the end of August German armoured vehicles were identified a few miles from the suburbs of Leningrad.

As parts of the German front stagnated and became increasingly embroiled in heavy fighting, Army Group North released its reserves including the Polizei Division. It was near Luga where the Polizei with the 269th Infantry Division became caught up in bitter fighting. Almost immediately units became disrupted and mired. Across the blasted front, troops became entangled in miles of earth walls, anti-tank ditches, wire barricades, dozens of defensive pill-boxes, and the harrying activities of Russian tanks. Soviet resistance was so strong that Polizei forces soon found themselves cut off in the wooded swampland. Determined not to be encircled and destroyed, the division, along with army formations, aggressively fought its way slowly to the north of Luga. It was here that Polizei showed its audacity and value on the battlefield. Against overwhelming odds, the division, supported by Heer formations, encircled and destroyed the Russian defenders. The battle around Luga, though successful, came at a heavy price. The division lost almost 2,000 soldiers including its commander, Arthur Mulverstadt, who was killed on 10 August by artillery fire.

Over the next days and weeks the Germans continued probing Russian resistance around Leningrad. The terrified civilians remaining inside the city walls were now going to endure one of the most brutal sieges in twentieth century history. They were given the depressing orders to defend their city to the death and not to surrender to the Nazi horde.

Although von Leeb's forces had arrived within shelling distance of Leningrad, the advance had not gone as planned. Regular Heer and Polizei units had been badly disrupted by heavy enemy resistance. Under increasing pressure from Hitler, they began a gigantic encirclement of the city, planned to join forces with the Finns, and annihilate the Soviet Baltic Fleet.

On 17 September the 41st Panzer Corps, which had managed to get into the outskirts of the city, was ordered by Hitler to pull out and move to the Moscow Front. Without the 41st Panzer Corps the whole dynamics of Army Group North quickly altered. There would now be no attack on Leningrad. Instead the Führer ordered that the city would be encircled and the inhabitants defending inside would be starved to death.

The Polizei Division was ordered to join the operation. Over the next few months Wehrmacht and Polizei forces dug in around Leningrad. During October and November 1941, some ten German divisions were tied down around the city.

(**Above**) Polizei troops have pressed a civilian cart into service, using it to transport men to a position. This photograph was taken while the division was in reserve during the opening stages of the German invasion of the Soviet Union. Much frivolity can be seen among the soldiers.

(**Opposite, above**) In reserve in Army Group North in East Prussia and these soldiers can be seen wearing their standard army greatcoats and M1938 field caps, tucking into breakfast.

(**Opposite, below**) A small HF12 small field kitchen wagon can be seen in a field and the men are being served rations while in reserve in late June 1941.

Four photographs taken in sequence showing a horse-drawn artillery Abteilung having difficulty negotiating a forest and a stream. The gun is a 10.5cm light field howitzer. The wheels on the artillery piece consisted of a heavy duty cast steel with a solid rubber rim. While the gun was almost invariably towed by animal draught, this type of design allowed the gun to be towed at relatively high speed by a motor vehicle. The 10.5cm field howitzer provided the division with a relatively effective mobile base of fire. It was primarily the artillery regiments that were given the task of destroying enemy positions and fortified defences and conducting counter-battery fire prior to an armoured assault.

(**Above**) Artillerymen with their horses pause in their march during the early phase of the invasion of Russia. The Polizei Division was part of von Leeb's Army Group North. Leeb was given the task of destroying the Red Army fighting in the Baltic region. It was to thrust across East Prussia, smashing Soviet positions along the Baltic, liquidating the bases of the Baltic Fleet, destroying what was left of Russian naval power, and capturing Kronstadt and Leningrad. Once the city had been razed to the ground, Leeb's force could sweep down from the north while the main force closed in from the west.

(**Opposite**) Two photographs taken in sequence showing Polizei during its advance towards Luga in early July 1941. In front of these units Wehrmacht troops of Army Group North were chewing through enemy positions heading through Lithuania, Latvia and Estonia, straight towards their objective – Leningrad. Under the blistering summer heat Leeb's army was able to advance rapidly through the Baltic states. By mid-July Army Group North had broken through south of Pskov and rolled toward Luga with Polizei bringing up the rear.

During an action near Luga in July 1941 and a Polizei mortar crew can be seen in action with their 8cm sGrW 34 mortar. It was common for infantry, especially during intensive long periods of action, to fire their mortar from either trenches or dug-in positions where the mortar crew could also be protected from enemy fire.

A soldier is seen inside a Zeltbahn tent while his comrade tucks into a biscuit and can be seen drinking from his canteen. The Zeltbahn, first issued in 1931, was a versatile piece of kit carried by each soldier. A number of them could be easily buttoned together to make a shelter or a tent.

Polizei troops have captured some large Soviet tracked howitzers during the battle of Luga. Some of the troops are wearing the Zeltbahn, being worn as a poncho over the field equipment. Each method of wearing the cape ensured that it gave the wearer the maximum amount of protection while at the same time allowed plenty of movement.

The cuff title of the 4 SS Polizei Division. Cuff titles had their origins in the nineteenth century. They were awarded as battle honours or to signify membership of an elite unit. However, during the Second World War this was not always the case. Several SS formations of dubious ability were awarded titles, as were several units which never came into existence, while others with good fighting reputations did not wear them. They were also issued to the personal training schools, command staffs or special formations.

(**Above**) Commanding officers confer with each other during an operation in July 1941. Two of the officers are wearing the army pattern field-grey greatcoat, which is identical to those worn by other ranks except for the reinforced leather patches to the shoulders indicating the rank, and the officers field cap.

(**Opposite, above**) A Polizei cyclist squad, or Radfahrer-Gruppe, pass a destroyed BT-7 Soviet light tank while operating in Army Group North. The radio antenna around the turret indicates that it was probably a command tank. The bulk of the Polizei at this time moved on foot at the pace of a soldier or plodding horse. However, these troops are equipped with troop bicycles 1938 or *Truppenfahrräder* 38, with which they could move quicker.

(**Opposite, below**) Polizei troops rest during their march on Luga in July 1941 wearing full battle kit. A vehicle can be seen halted next to them serving as a medical car with a red marker cross painted on a white square background.

Polizei troops guide a horse through deep water pulling a limber across a muddy stream in the summer of 1941.

(**Opposite, above**) Troops march past a dead Russian soldier sprawled out across a forest track. The Polizei found the Baltic republics and adjoining Russian territory to be heavily forested. Troops who fought in these forested regions seldom penetrated very deeply while on patrol, partly due to the difficulty of movement but also for fear of ambush. The soldiers are wearing mosquito nets.

(**Opposite, below**) Photographed by the Polizei showing a muddy Pz.Kpfw.IV halted on a road following a heavy downpour of rain. Between 1936 and 1945, over 8,000 Pz.Kpfw.IVs were built. For most of the war this tank was a match for its opponent's heavy tanks and quickly and effectively demonstrated its superiority on the battlefield.

(**Opposite, above**) Polizei troops limber up a captured Russian 76 M1927 anti-tank gun. Both sides used each other's weapons.

(**Above**) Polizei soldiers pay their respects at an army grave during a pause in the fighting on the Leningrad front. The Leningrad front was first formed by the Soviet army on 23 August 1941 by dividing the Northern front into the Leningrad and Karelian fronts during the German approach on Leningrad. It stretched from the Gulf of Finland to Lake Ilmen and into Estonia. Russian resistance was fierce and there were many Germans casualties.

(**Opposite, below**) The crew of a 7.5cm le.IG18 out in a field during an action. Although the gun was one of the first post-First World War weapons to be issued to the Wehrmacht, it remained in service throughout the war. The weapon has steel discs with pneumatic tyres suggesting that it has been towed to its position by a vehicle. The use of pneumatic tyres reduced wear and tear and allowed the gun to be transported quicker.

Men of an SS-Flak-Abteilung tuck into their rations during a pause in their march. While equipment in 1941 for the Polizei was still limited, the division's flak consisted mainly of small numbers of 8.8cm, 5cm and 3.7cm flak guns.

An interesting photograph showing special flatbed rail cars carrying Polizei limbers and artillery caissons on a special wide-gauge railway line. Note all the straw for the horses strewn next to the wooden rail platform. It can only be imagined the logistics of using animal draught on the Eastern Front. The German Army alone had brought some 800,000 horses to the front in the summer of 1941.

Two blurred photographs taken in sequence during an enemy action showing the artillery crew while on a fire mission with their 10.5cm 1.FH 18 field howitzer. The 10.5cm howitzer had a nine-man crew. Usually fewer are seen serving this piece because often some of the crew were to the rear with the horses, limber and caisson.

(**Above**) A captured French Schneider 155mm C mie 1917 on the Leningrad Front being used by Polizei. The Germans designated this gun 15.5cm s.FH 414 (f). It was used primarily as a defence gun.

(**Opposite**) An interesting photograph showing captured a French Schneider 220mm mie 1916 breech loading mortar being used during the siege of Leningrad. The Germans designated this weapon as a 22cm Mrs 53 (f).

(**Below**) A battery of 10.5cm le.FH 18s in their firing position in a field. There were four guns to a battery, as in this photograph, but as the war in the east progressed and there were high losses, surviving guns were occasionally consolidated into larger batteries.

Polizei troops are seen standing next to a Pz.Kpfw.III on a road in northern Russia. The region had vast lakes, swamps and forested areas, and tanks and other vehicles often found their progress hindered by soft marshy ground and lack of good roads.

Advancing through the mud. Artillery crewman were sometimes unable to ride on the caisson and limber to keep weight down.

Polizei troops help push a vehicle along a muddy track. Muddy conditions on the Eastern front during operations in 1941 plagued the front. By this period the weather began to change. Within hours of a downpour the Russian countryside had been turned into a quagmire with roads and fields becoming virtually impassable. Many of the roads leading to the front had become boggy swamps. Although tanks and other tracked vehicles managed to push through the mire at slow pace, animal draft, trucks and other wheeled vehicles became hopelessly stuck in deep boggy mud.

A PaK crew with their 5cm PaK 38. The PaK 38 was well liked among the crews. Not only was the weapon effective in combat, but also easy to conceal. It was the first anti-tank weapon to be produced as full-sized artillery. Although they proved deadly against French and British armour in 1940, by the time they saw action in Russia a year later, German gunners soon realized they needed a more potent anti-tank gun.

A 10.5cm howitzer's caisson and limber struggle across a muddy field. Each artillery piece with its own limber was accompanied by a caisson with additional ammunition equipment. Between the artillery piece and caisson a single gun required twelve draft horses and was serviced by a nine-man crew.

Soldiers of the Polizei Division move along a road that has been submerged following heavy rain in September 1941. Most roads were no more than dirt tracks that often disappeared into a boggy quagmire which even tanks were unable to handle. Germans on foot sank past the top of their black leather boots and horses sank to their bellies.

In the autumn of 1941 spread out across a field a number of regiments belonging to Polizei can be seen. The division has captured some fortified positions comprising bunkers and trenches and are regrouping following its successful engagement.

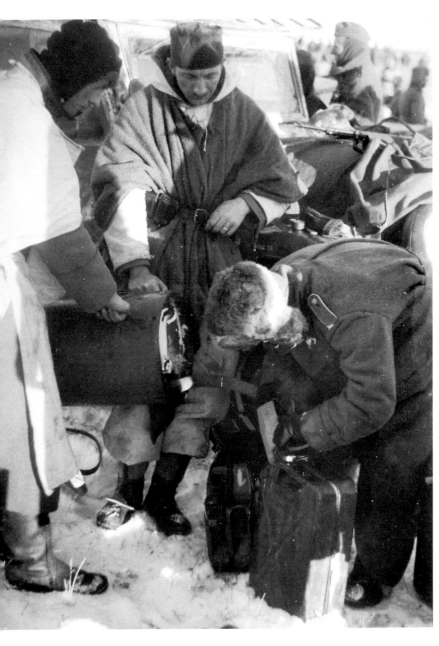

Fuel and oil kept the front lines from grinding to a complete halt. Here Polizei troops are collecting fuel in their twenty-litre fuel tanks. Note the lack of basic winter clothing for these soldiers. The soldier in the middle of the picture wears a blanket over his shoulders, held in place by his black leather belt. The other two men wear the standard greatcoat with one wearing the early white camouflage shirt.

(**Opposite, above**) Members of the Polizei undergo an inspection parade inside a forest during winter operations. The Soviet offensive in August had been gruelling, with German forces fighting a series of bloody battles to hold their positions on the Leningrad front. The Germans had managed to blunt the Soviet penetrations through their lines with the sacrifice of thousands of men killed and wounded.

(**Opposite, below**) Men of the Polizei can be seen erecting shelters inside a forest during winter operations. When the temperature rapidly dropped at the end of October, these shelters were a lifeline. Troops that did not have adequate shelter often froze to death.

(**Above**) Polizei troops trudge along a snowy path on the Leningrad front in the winter of 1941. The men lack the basics for winter warfare with all of them still wearing the standard Wehrmacht-issue great coat. A few wear the snow shirts which were intended only to conceal the soldier and not to keep him warm.

(**Opposite, above**) Here Polizei ski-troops wear the snow overall. This white garment was an early piece of snow clothing. It was long, covering the entire service uniform, and was designed to reach the wearer's ankles. It was shapeless, had buttons right down the front, a deep collar, an attached hood and long sleeves. The black infantryman's leather belt and personal equipment was worn attached around the outside of the garment to allow better access. All the soldiers are wearing a coloured armband on their left arm, which enabled German troops to distinguish between friend and foe. Generally the colour armband was green, but it could be changed in colour or position depending on the frequently changing security sequence.

(**Opposite, below**) Polizei ski troops wearing the snow overall during a pause in a reconnaissance mission in late 1941. Skis were an effective means of movement across frozen terrain, and were used extensively by reconnaissance patrols.

Ski troops during a reconnaissance mission have halted in the snow while one observes the terrain through a pair of 6 × 30 binoculars. They all wear the snow overall and are armed with a Kar 98k bolt-action rifle. There had been little preparation made at high levels of command to outfit German soldiers with the appropriate clothing, weapons and food to withstand the horrors of a Russian winter. Instead, the troops had to adapt to stay alive.

In a defensive position inside a trench in a forest on the Leningrad front Polizei troops can be seen clad in their winter whites. All of them wear their M35 steel helmets, two of them have their head gear in white, while the soldier on the left has his helmet in the original slate grey.

Inside a Russian village in the winter of 1941 and a group of Polizei pose for the camera standing, unusually, behind a gramophone. They wear the M38 field cap, M36 field blouse with its typical dark-green facing collar, and M40 field service trousers. Only one wears the standard army-issue greatcoat.

An infantry gun crew with their 7.5cm le.IG18 out on the Leningrad front in the winter of 1941. These small light highly mobile infantry guns were more than capable of providing German troops with offensive and defensive fire support, particularly when heavier artillery was unavailable. Note the discarded ammunition cases suggesting this gun has been engaged in a fire mission.

Chapter Four

Bitter Fighting
(1942)

By January 1942, the situation only got worse as temperatures plummeted, preventing any kind of movement against the enemy. To make matters worse the Red Army began an offensive, and consequently put many German units onto the defensive. As troops clashed in the snow, the Polizei Division was given official Waffen-SS status. Its title was changed to the SS Polizei-Division and all the division's sub-units were renamed.

The SS Polizei-Division saw heavy fighting along the Volkhov River. Along the winding river banks, swamp lands and dense forests, the Red Army believed that they would be able to regain the initiative and push back the German military machine in Russia.

But Stalin and his commanders were over confident and underestimated German determination. What followed along the Volkhov River was a bloody battle of attrition as German forces contested every inch of ground and fought to the death defending their positions. Soviets were compelled to quickly call up reinforcements. The Wehrmacht then aggressively counter-attacked with air support. It did not take long before Red Army formations found themselves encircled and were battered into submission by ground and aerial attacks. Soviet formations attempted to breakout of the encirclement, but the Wehrmacht, including the Polizei, closed in to seal the enemy's fate. Hundreds of German guns of all calibres poured a storm of fire onto Soviet positions. In the face of overwhelming force the Russians finally ordered all offensive manoeuvres to halt, and attempts were made to escape the encirclement. As soldiers of the 2nd Soviet Shock Army tried to escape, the Luftwaffe stepped up its operations, while Polizei quickly shifted north to block their exit.

The defeat of the Red Army along the smoldering banks of the Volkhov had brought confidence back to the German commanders, but this would be short lived. Operations in Army Group North were unpredictable, and the Soviet Army still had tremendous reserves to call upon.

Over the next weeks and months the front, almost six hundred miles long, moved slightly east, and then more or less came to a grinding halt. From the Baltic, around the siege perimeter at Leningrad, due south to Lake Ilmen, and then across the often dense pine forests at Rzhev and down to Orel, the German front stagnated. A sense of futility and gloom began to grip the German soldier in the north. Thousands of troops had been killed, and by mid-October 1942, they found themselves substantially in the same position they had been in spring. From the Volkhov River to the Gulf of Finland the front was reminiscent of the First World War, with a string of trenches and shell holes in which gains and losses could be measured only in yards. Because of defeats in southern Russia, German forces were now compelled to go on the defensive. Despite the daily shelling, Leningrad gradually regained strength and became a fortress capable of withstanding a further year and a half of siege and every enemy attempt to destroy it. It also managed to pin down most of Army Group North which was desperately needed elsewhere to plug the crumbling fronts.

As for the Polizei Division, it manned its lines night and day, which were often quiet for many days at a time. When winter once more set in, the desolate terrain occasionally erupted with bands of partisans on horseback attacking German billets far behind the lines. Polizei ski troops repeatedly sent out scout patrols to harass the enemy and to locate their positions.

The troops, while still regarded as second-rate SS, had received winter whites and additional winter clothing. They had built log and earth shelters and had established for themselves almost comfortable living conditions.

But by the end of 1942 the Russians were now definitely the stronger force.

A column of horse-drawn transport pulling supplies, weapons and other provisions on the march during the early winter of 1942. Movement for the Polizei during the winter period around Leningrad had almost stagnated.

Winter operation in early 1942 and ski troops on a patrol, wearing their distinctive two-piece white camouflage smocks and whitewashed steel helmets, prepare to move out. Note the 7.5cm le.IG18 with pneumatic tyres which can just be seen on the right of the photograph.

An interesting photograph showing a mixture of Heer, Polizei and Gebirgsjäger troops on the march with a whitewashed Pz.Kpfw.III, prior to regrouping. The distances over which the soldiers had to travel were immense. Wheeled transportation was generally useless in the trackless wastes and forests, and often the most effective means of transport was tracked vehicles, sleds or skis.

(**Above**) Inside a captured town and infantry take to a shelter as an air raid warning sounds. Soviet fighters and bombers regularly dropped incendiary bombs on shelters used by the Germans. This could include complete villages and towns, which were devastated without regard for the cost to their inhabitants. As a result of this, Heer and SS troops often chose to live out in the open, although living in extreme temperatures without shelter caused problems for the men and equipment.

(**Opposite**) Two photographs taken in sequence showing a whitewashed 10.5cm le.FH 18. The gun crew have draped a white sheet over one of the wheels and its gun barrel for camouflage and to make it harder for enemy reconnaissance crews to work what weapon the Germans are using. In the second photograph the crew have a applied a sapling for additional camouflage protection. Note that they are also cleaning the breech block and have removed the firing pin.

(**Opposite, above**) Polizei troops strap an injured soldier to the sidecar of a motorcycle combination during the division's withdrawal. They are all wearing their white camouflage suits which blend well with the local countryside.

(**Opposite, below**) A Polizei gun crew pose for the camera with a captured Soviet 122mm M1938 howitzer. This artillery piece was one of the most reliable and well-liked weapons used in the Russian arsenal during the war. The crewman on the right with double chevrons stitched on his left sleeve and left collar patch is an SS-Rottenführer.

(**Above**) A 10.5cm battery has moved out and is on the march across a field. Normally an artillery Abteilung moved out in intervals with one or two always in position to give supporting fire. Their positions may have been overwhelmed and the safest option for the gun crews was an immediate evacuation of the area.

A 10.5cm gun crew pose with their weapon. It is presumed that due to the lack of camouflage on the howitzer the crew will only be in this position for a short period. Note the crew wearing the early-style SS fur cap.

An injured Polizei soldier is evacuated during the unit's withdrawal. Note the unit's inscription stencilled on the side of the sled.

Troops on the march with a halftrack towing a supply wagon through water during the thaw in April 1942. The spring thaw of 1942 was another hindrance to the German war machine in Russia. Mud and water often caused huge delays in moving men and equipment from one part of the front to another.

A 10.5cm howitzer crew being moved to another part of the front with the rest of its Abteilung. Note the crew members wearing mosquito nets. Mosquitoes were a constant problem for the men in the spring and summer periods in northern Russia. Also note the large sacks behind the gun piece which contains horse fodder.

(**Above**) A 10.5cm Abteilung on the march during the spring thaw in 1942. As can be seen, the roads in Russia quickly became very muddy due to the high volumes of traffic. Note to the right of the photograph a motorcycle combination crew trying to move their vehicle out of the mire after it has evidently become stuck.

(**Opposite, above**) An interesting photograph showing what looks to be a hastily erected command post using a commandeered cart. The cart has been heavily camouflaged with straw. Note the leather map board on the soldier's back, while a leather map tube can be seen positioned on the right. The soldier is seen carrying his woollen bed roll blanket.

(**Opposite, below**) Here is one of the many narrow-gauge railways that were used by the Germans to transport armour and equipment quickly from one part of the front to another, to avoid the long distances travelled across often rough terrain. In this photograph a battery of 10.5cm howitzers have been loaded on board a narrow-gauge train, nicknamed 'Flitzkopp'.

(**Above**) A well decorated SS standard leader, or SS-Standartenführer, who was in charge of a regiment-sized unit can be seen conferring with his men in a defensive position on the front line.

(**Opposite, above**) From the same defensive position a troop leader can be seen with his back to the camera with an MP40 and gas mask canister slung round his back. The same commander holding the rank of an SS-Standartenführer has just lit a cigarette during a pause in the fighting. Behind them is a stationary halftrack prime mover and a Pz.Kpfw.III. Note the devastation as far as the eye can see.

(**Opposite, below**) A command post near Rzhev. Three of the commanders on the left of the photograph hold the rank of SS senior assault leaders, or SS-Obersturmführer. By this period Polizei had officially integrated into the Waffen-SS as the SS-Polizei-Division. Army/Police uniforms/insignia were replaced with Waffen-SS equivalents. However, the division continued to wear the police emblem.

(**Above**) Soldiers of the SS-Polizei-Division during an operation in the summer of 1942. Over the next weeks and months the front moved slightly east, and then stagnated again. For almost 600 miles, the front more or less came to a grinding halt. From the Baltic, around the siege perimeter at Leningrad, due south to Lake Ilmen, and then across the often dense pine forests at Rzhev and down to Orel, the German front hardly moved.

(**Opposite**) Polizei troops on the march in the summer of 1942. One soldier appears to be holding an MG42 machine gun slung over his shoulder. All the men display an excellent array of infantryman's combat equipment. Attached to their black leather belt is their mess kit and shelter quarter. They have their canteen, bread bag, which carried rations as well as small personal items, and their gas mask canister. Often the mask itself was discarded and the robust and waterproof canister was used to carry personal items the soldier wanted to keep dry such as tobacco, letters, and photographs. Note to the right of the men are Soviet PoWs encamped behind a small barbed-wire fence.

Next to a large lake in Army Group North is evidently a 10.5cm howitzer unit. Note the number of support wagons and support vehicles employed to maintain an efficient Abteilung. Many of the men can be seen in their swimming wear, and no doubt the horses have enjoyed a much-earned respite in the water.

Decorated with the Iron Cross during a decoration ceremony is an SS assault platoon leader, or SS-Sturmscharführer. Note the cuff title of the 4th SS-Polizei-Division. Most of these cuff titles were black cloth with silver gothic lettering and silver edging.

Two photographs showing an MG34 machine gun on an anti-aircraft tripod. The assistant gunner stands next to the M41 ammunition box which held five 50-round belts of ammunition. Note the Zeltbahn draped over the tripod which was used for concealment and to help protect the gunner when it rained.

(**Opposite, above**) A light battery of 10.5cm le.FH 18 artillery pieces in a field. The three light artillery battalions each had three four-gun batteries with 10.5cm howitzers. A battalion would usually be placed in direct support of an infantry regiment, but did not belong to the regiment.

(**Opposite, below**) During operations in late 1942 and two riflemen can be seen in a dug-in position. The soldier on the right is armed with the 7.92mm Kar98k bolt-action Mauser, the standard-issue German rifle of the war. Both men are wearing hooded reversible jackets with their camouflage suit over it. The jacket was specifically worn by the Waffen-SS. It was the first truly reversible winter weather uniform and offered the men both extra warmth and concealment.

(**Above**) Along the same defensive position is a photograph of one of the same soldiers as in photo 28. He is seen wearing the hooded jacket, trousers and mittens. The material used for the uniform was padded insulating material with water-repellent fabric outer shell. This photograph was taken in 1942 as the troops are wearing the fur-lined winter hoods which were introduced during this period to front line troops.

Polizei troops can be seen wearing the early style SS fur cap. While one of the soldiers on the left is wearing the standard-issue greatcoat over his M36 service issue uniform, his comrades are all wearing the new hooded reversible jacket with fur-lined hood.

SS troops are aiding an injured comrade on a stretcher. While one of the soldiers is wearing the early type white camouflage garment, two men can be seen wearing the animal skin greatcoat over their army field service uniform. This garment was excellent for keeping warm. However, being light coloured they quickly got dirty.

A soldier gives a Nazi salute to his commanding officer who holds a leather map case as he departs back to his divisional headquarters. The officer, who holds the rank of SS-Standartenführer, is wearing gold collar patches with a Knight's Cross pinned to the neck of his tunic. Attached to his grey-green leather greatcoat with reinforced leather patches to the shoulders are gold cording braid shoulder straps.

From the unit's field quarters troops pose for the camera with a sidecar combination. Although the Polizei fought hard to hold its positions, they were constantly subjected to intense enemy ground bombardments in the region around Lake Ladoga. Difficulties in terrain hindered movement and communication between the units and defences were often thinly spread, which allowed the Soviets plenty of weak spots through which to infiltrate.

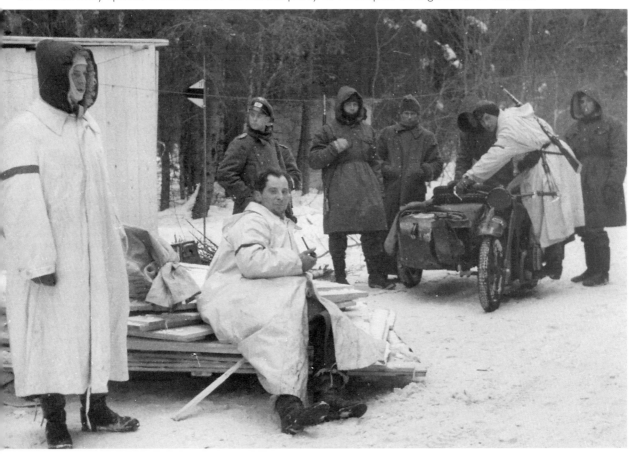

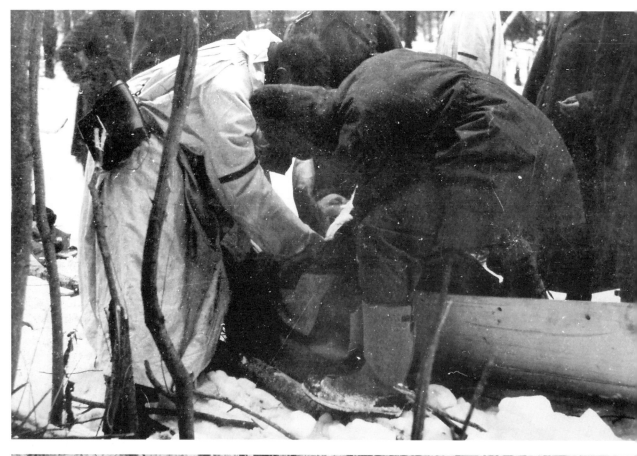

(**Above and following**) The first of four photographs showing wide-gauge railway line platforms and Polizei troops unloading weapons, equipment and horses from the special flatcars. The low-profile platforms were specially designed to have small gaps between the flatcars and platform so that items could be easily entrained or detrained. All the images show Artillerie Abteilung 4 unloading 10.5cm howitzers from the flatcars and limbering them up for front line service. The fourth photograph shows howitzers and caissons awaiting the arrival of the narrow-gauge train to pull up alongside the specially built timber platform so that the crew can entrain to another part of the battlefield. It was quite common for the Germans to move all their units from one place to another by train. In fact it was often undertaken so quickly that the enemy frequently did not detect movement of the Germans withdrawing and being transported to another part of the front until reconnaissance later found them positioned somewhere else.

(**Opposite, above**) Troops assist an injured comrade in the snow and have loaded him onto a sled, securing him in place for his journey to a field hospital.

(**Opposite, below**) A soldier makes the most of the natural environment by constructing a makeshift shelter in the forest to keep warm from the bitter arctic conditions. Sheltering out in the snow sometimes proved difficult. By 1942 German soldiers were being taught to construct native-style shelters from tree branches and even build igloos.

Polizei troops can be seen with a knocked-out Russian tank. The men onboard the tank are dressed in the now popular SS winter uniform comprising hooded jacket, trousers and mittens. The uniform was reversible and in this photograph they are clearly wearing it grey-side out.

(**Above and following**) The first of five photographs taken in sequence showing Artillerie Abteilung 4 moving from one position to another using animal draught in the snow. It shows the difficulties artillery crews had transporting their equipment during the winter. The terrain was also difficult for the animals which in these extreme conditions often became exhausted, as seen in one of the photographs. Most of the soldiers are dressed in the SS winter hooded jacket, trousers and mittens.

(**Opposite, above**) Troops digging in preparing their position for a fire mission in the snow with their PaK 7.5cm l.IG18 guns. These small light highly mobile infantry guns were more than capable of providing troops with offensive and defensive fire support, particularly when heavy artillery was unavailable.

(**Opposite, below**) Out in the snow is a whitewashed 8.8cm Flak 18 gun being readied by its crew for action. This was the most famous German anti-aircraft gun of the war. It was bolted onto a cruciform platform from which it fired with outriggers extended. Here in this photograph the crew have used the weapon in a ground attack role. On the battlefield it proved a very versatile weapon and continued being used in a dual role until the end of the war. Note the gun's limber positioned nearby. The limber were normally positioned like this in order for the crews to rapidly limber up and reposition the gun.

Two photographs taken in sequence showing two officers. The officer dressed in a greatcoat is an SS-Hauptsturmführer, the other is an SS-Untersturmführer. He wears the Iron Cross 1st Class and a wound badge on his left breast pocket.

On the front line on Christmas Day and an artillery crew pose for the camera with one of the men holding a bottle of alcohol in his hand in a makeshift shelter in the snow. Of interest is that projectile packing frames have been used to help build the shelter. Note in the distance is a large staff tent probably sheltering the battery headquarters (*Batterie Truppe*).

Posing for the camera kitted out in their winter clothing in the snow in late 1942 is a security patrol. Artillery units were often expected to provide their own local security and defence, and these men were detailed to protect them. The men are armed with the Karabiner 98K bolt-action rifle. Note the M24 stick grenades stuck into their black leather SS belts.

Chapter Five

Greece and the Eastern Front (1943–1945)

Army Group North in early 1943 was under increasing pressure from the Red Army. Polizei and Heer watched anxiously from their relatively inactive front. Commanders in the field were well aware that if the hold on Leningrad were broken, Army Group North would lose control of the Baltic Sea. Finland would be isolated; supplies of iron ore from Sweden would be in danger, and the U-boat training programme would be seriously curtailed. It was imperative that the troops held the front until other parts of the Russian front could be stabilized.

Yet the fighting in the east was already at breaking point. Although there were plans for various offensives, generally the war in Russia was a defensive one. The front lines were now denuded of proper equipment, and troops and armour were thinly spread out on the battlefield. On 12 January 1943 the Russians launched the second battle of Lake Ladoga, which began with an artillery bombardment of 4,000 guns lasting for an hour. Then the Soviet 2nd Shock Army advanced, smashing into the German front line and causing considerable casualties. The Polizei Division fought off several determined Russian attacks. At Kolpino it successfully held its line despite suffering many more casualties.

Under strength and badly mauled by the fierce fighting around Kolpino, the division were removed from operations in Army Group North and transported west to recuperate and retrain. To support dwindling front line units in the east, the division did leave behind a small Kampfgruppe and this was strengthened by a new Dutch Volunteer Legion Niederlande. The Legion and the Polizei Kampfgruppe were engaged in defensive operations until May 1943, often in appalling conditions, from fortified positions manned with Pak guns and lines of machine gun pits.

In early June the division was converted as motorized and renamed as the SS-Polizei-Panzergrenadier Division. In July two regiments were sent to the Balkans for what was called 'security measures'. In Greece the Polizei undertook anti-partisan operations in the northern part of the country. It was here in the Greek countryside that the SS began a clearance operation and a demonstration of dominance against the civilian population. Over the coming months the Polizei roamed the hills and mountains trying with varying degrees of success to flush out resistance fighters.

In September 1943, the division was sent south of Belgrade for training and to protect against a possible Allied invasion of the Balkans. A month later, units joined part of the 22nd Army Corps in anti-partisan activities in an operation code-named Panther, which involved clearing the Jannina-Metsovo road in Greece of Elas guerrillas. SS and army troops were ordered to show no mercy, to either fighters or civilians. The partisans were undeterred by the German operation and demonstrated courage which often led to reckless sacrifice. Again and again the Germans showed there were no limits to their ruthlessness as they obeyed orders.

In December some of the division, now with a strength of over 16,000 men, was posted to Salonika, while the main body of Polizei carried on with anti-partisan operations in Greece. On the Eastern Front the Polizei Kampfgruppe was relieved by the SS Panzergrenadier Brigade Niederlande while part of the Polizei's artillery remained at the Oranienbaum bridgehead in support. Fighting in the area was heavy, and losses high.

By 15 January 1944, the defences along the front in the north were finally attacked by three powerful Soviet fronts: the Leningrad, Volkhov and Second Baltic. The 18th Army, which bore the brunt of the main attacks, were outnumbered by at least 3:1. As usual German troops were expected to hold the front, but overwhelming enemy firepower proved too much for Kuechler's Army Group and it was compelled to fall back.

By 26 January the city of Leningrad was liberated after nine hundred days of siege. The 18th Army was now split into three parts and struggled to hold any type of front forward of the Luga River. During March the Russians began exerting more pressure, especially against the 16th Army that was defending positions along the Baltic. But the spring thaw had arrived early and melting snow had turned the roads on which the Russians were travelling into a quagmire. The conditions were so bad that forward units from the 16th Army reported that Soviet tanks could be seen sinking up to their turrets in mud. It seemed the front lines were temporarily holding, with the weather playing a major part in containing the Red Army.

In March the division operated around Salonika and clashed with a number of partisans. Over the following days and weeks anti-partisan operations intensified and Polizei became more hostile against the local population, blaming it for aiding the partisan activities. On 10 June, soldiers of the division under the command of SS-Hauptsturmführer Fritz Lautenbach, rounded up Greek civilians in Distomo. They hanged and shot over 200 of them, including women and children, in what they called 'a retaliation measure for a partisan attack'. Distomo was not an isolated incident, and in nearby towns and villages the Polizei undertook other barbaric actions including murdering babies and a pregnant woman. They beheaded a village priest near Delphi;

in the mountains of central Greece they murdered twenty-eight civilians in Ypati; and they razed Spercheiada and countless other villages to the ground in numerous vengeance attacks.

In September the division was pulled out of Greece and rushed to take part in fighting around the city of Timișoara in Romania where a German garrison was holding out. Polizei, Heer and Hungarian troops attempted to take the city by force but without success. The garrison inside the city surrendered and Polizei were quickly withdrawn and shifted to a defensive action against Red Army forces at Drobeta-Turnu Severin. This city had been encircled by strong Soviet forces, and Polizei together with other units managed to allow the 1st Gebirgsjäger-Division to escape.

Polizei then fought in the Banat region and fought a series of counter-attacks against Russian advances at Horgos on the Romanian and Hungarian border. Russian forces pushed forward, captured the Zombor region, and pushed the Polizei Division into Slovakia in early January 1945.

On 26 January the division was moved from Hungary to Army Group Vistula in Pomerania. This group was mainly formed of Wehrmacht forces put together from surviving remnants of Army Group A, Army Group Centre, and a variety of ad hoc formations including Hitlerjugend conscripts and various other local militia and volunteers. Its main purpose was to protect Berlin from the Soviet Army advancing from the Vistula River.

Despite the best efforts of the German Army to bolster its dwindling ranks on the Eastern Front during the last months of the war, nothing could mask the fact that they were dwarfed by the superiority of the Red Army. It was estimated that the Russians had some six million men along a front which stretched from the Adriatic to the Baltic. To the German soldiers facing the Russians as they battled through East Prussia withdrawing across into West Prussia and Pomerania, the outcome was almost certain death.

On 15 March the Second Belorussian Front opened an offensive along the Baltic thrusting its powerful force towards the coast at Zoppot between Gotenhafen and Danzig. In order to avert the capture of these towns, Colonel General Walter Weiss quickly pulled together a force to defend the area consisting of the VII Panzer-Korps, XXXXV Armee-Korps, XXVII Armee-Korps, 251 Infantry-Division, 4 SS-Polizei, 7 Panzer-Division , 215 Infantry-Division, 32 Infantry-Division, 227 Infantry-Division, 73 Infantry-Division, 389 Infantry-Division and 252 Infantry-Division.

In the Arnswalde the VII Panzer-Korps, together with Polizei, were ordered to blunt the Russian drive. However, while it appeared that the Germans were prepared for a Soviet attack, much of the equipment employed along the defensive belts was too thinly spread. Commanders too were unable to predict where the strategic focal point of the Soviet attack would be. Then the Russians began bombarding German positions all along the frontier. Under-armed, units of the VII Panzer-Korps were driven from their defensive positions and pulverised. When some determined units refused to budge, the Russians ordered in their flamethrowers to burn them out.

Remnants of the Polizei Division then temporarily saw action around Hela under Army Group East Prussia, until evacuated to Swinemünde. The seaport there was heavily defended by Fortress Division Swinemünde. It was an important naval base and home to the German rocket facility. Forming the northern anchor of the 3rd Panzer Army, the Fortress Division was used to protect the northern shores of the Baltic against the advancing Red Army. For weeks the fortress held out while the Soviets occupied large areas around the port.

Swinemünde was encircled by the Soviet 2nd Belorussian Front. When the evacuation of the port was ordered, elements of the Polizei escaped and advanced towards Berlin, but by this time the Red Army had already encircled the doomed Reichs capital. Any chance of Polizei stragglers getting into the city was almost gone and some perished attempting to break through. Others surrendered to US troops at Wittenberge-Lenzen. The remnants left at Swinemünde were all killed or escaped to Denmark where they were taken captive by the British Army.

The Polizei Division had led an extraordinary existence on the battlefield. It had made its debut on the Western Front in 1940, it had bled in Russia a year later, fought a number of defensive battles in 1943, and undertook extensive partisan operations in Greece. A few months later in early 1945, the remnants of its force battled its way across East Prussia in the defence of the Battle of the Baltic, and fought a number of isolated encounters until it was either destroyed or captured. But Polizei had tainted its war record with monstrous crimes against humanity, which will never be forgotten, or indeed forgiven.

Various halftracks can be seen scattered across a snow-covered field during winter operations in January 1943. These front-wheel-steering vehicles with tracked drive were vital for the Heer and the SS for transporting troops, ordnance and supplies to the front. Variants included command vehicles, communication vehicles, artillery carriers, multiple rocket launchers, anti-aircraft platforms, and anti-tank weapons carriers.

A gunner stands next to his 7.5cm PaK40. This gun was a compact design and when dug-in and well concealed, it presented a very small frontal silhouette. Like the PaK38, the PaK40 also had a spaced-armour shield held together by large bolts.

A blurry image showing support vehicles out in the field during early winter operations on the Eastern Front in 1943. Both vehicles, surprisingly, retain their summer camouflage scheme of dark yellow with red brown and olive green vertical and wavy stripes.

Though not totally clear, it is evident in this photograph that part of the shelter comprising a straw and grass roof is smoking and being cleared by troops to stop it bursting into flames. The roof has probably been in contact with incendiary material or hot shrapnel from a nearby projectile blast.

Early winter operations in 1943 and Pz.Kpfw.IIIs are using nearby hut-like dwellings as cover from enemy ground surveillance. In the distance other vehicles too are using buildings as cover.

(**Opposite, above**) An interesting photograph showing Polizei troops with a drop container known as a supply bomb container or Nachschubbombe. These 'bomb drop containers' were often parachuted along the front to quickly supplement the troops with urgent equipment and rations.

(**Opposite, below**) A Polizei soldier inside a trench with local Russian men drafted in as 'helpers'. These 'helpers' were brought in to support soldiers on the front and rear lines, bringing up supplies and equipment and tending to horses. This soldier is part of a Polizei Kampfgruppe that was strengthened by a Dutch Volunteer Legion Niederlande. They were engaged in defensive operations in mid-1943 on the Eastern Front. During this period the troops endured appalling conditions, and along the front they were experiencing defensive problems in many areas, in spite of strong fortified positions.

(**Above**) Two photographs showing Polizei troops along one of the many defensive positions west of Kolpino in mid-1943. A trench periscope can be seen overlooking a position. The periscope was an optical device for conducting observations from a concealed protected position. The device was especially effective during trench or urban fighting where soldiers often had to endure many hours or days in the same fixed or fortified position.

(**Above**) Inside a trench and a shirtless rifleman armed with a Karabiner 98k bolt-action rifle can be seen aiming his weapon at a suspected target. Note a child's toy doll and the pair of black leather marching boots to his left.

(**Opposite**) Along one of the many trenches that were dug along the Eastern Front in Army Group North officers can be seen. One officer is an SS-Brigadeführer and holds a 1st Class Iron Cross pinned to his neck. The other officer is a SS-Untersturmführer. Note the Sf14Z scissor periscope. Although the periscope, commonly known as 'donkey ears', was able to estimate ranges, it provided a narrow field of vision.

(**Above and opposite, above**) Two photographs showing Polizei officers during anti-partisan sweeps in Greece in 1943. It was here in the Greek countryside that soldiers of the Polizei Division began a brutal and terrifying clearance operation.

(**Opposite, below**) A group of Polizei troops on a Greek mountain road in 1943. A motorcycle combination and a Horch cross-country car can be seen halted on a road. The partisan war in Greece was fought with great ferocity on both sides, and SS units were guilty of atrocities.

An officer, wearing the popular rubberized motorcycle coat over his uniform, confers with his staff during operations in Greece in 1944.

(**Opposite, above**) Polizei troops rest during partisan operations in 1943. The majority of Polizei troops' insignia were replaced with SS insignia, but photographic evidence such as this suggests it was a slow process as front-line troops had more pressing issues to deal with first. The men still retain their M35 steel helmets with camouflage helmet covering, and the M40 field blouse. Over this garment is worn the plain tree SS camouflage M40 reversible, showing it in spring/summer camouflage. They all wear the standard infantryman's field equipment.

(**Opposite, below**) Two SS-Scharführer, or section leaders, playing a game of chess in northern Greece. Their M40 field blouse has been replaced by the new Waffen-SS insignia. It displays the SS runes and rank collar patches. Their field grey army shoulder straps have been replaced by the Waffen-SS black type.

Weapons and equipment can be seen onboard the special railway flatcars in Greece in 1944. Note foliage has been attached to help conceal the cargo and for camouflage.

An SS-Sturmmann, or SS-assault man or stormtrooper, on the left wearing the SS M40 field blouse and displaying SS runes and rank collar patches. His comrade on the right is an SS-Unterscharführer, or SS-junior section leader. Worn over his SS M40 field blouse is plain tree SS camouflage M40 reversible. Both men wear the summer camouflage M43 field cap.

An officer can be seen holding a bunch of grapes with his motorcycle combination. Because of the hot climate soldiers during operations in Greece often did not wear the full service uniform but instead tended to wear the tropical field trousers and the tropical shirt. The shirt was hard wearing and was made of cotton drill dyed to a darkish sand colour. It was primarily designed to take the place of the tropical field service tunic.

A time to cool with water in the hot climate during a pause in the unit's move through Greece in 1944.

Three commanding officers can be seen conferring on a road in Greece in 1944. The officers on the left and in the middle are ranked SS-Obersturmführer while the officer on the right is an SS-Obersturmbannführer.

Another photograph of the same SS-Obersturmbannführer driving a vehicle in Greece in 1944. He has been decorated with a Knight's Cross.

An SS-Sturmbannführer with his horse during anti-partisan duties in Greece.

Four photographs showing the same Polizei unit during an anti-partisan patrol in northern Greece in 1944. All the men are wearing camouflage smocks over their M40 blouses, some displaying SS collar patches and SS rank insignia, while others still retain their original collar patches. Over the weeks and months the Polizei roamed the hills and mountains trying with varying degrees of success to flush out resistance fighters. Operations gradually intensified, and the Polizei became more hostile against the local population, blaming it for aiding partisan activities. They committed some of the most barbaric crimes in the history of the Waffen-SS.

(**Above**) Commanding officers are seen with a Fieseler Storch which appears to be packed with a lot of cargo. The Storch was a small German liaison aircraft and was used extensively during the war.

(**Opposite**) Two photographs taken during a visit to a Pomeranian airfield by commanding officers during the last months of the war in 1945. By early February 1945 German forces in the east had been driven back to the River Oder, the last bastion of defence before Berlin. Only three weeks earlier, the Eastern Front was still deep in Poland. Now Upper Silesia was lost; in East Prussia German forces were smashed to pieces; West Prussia and Pomerania were being defended by depleted troops thrown together, and the defence of the Oder was now being entrusted to exhausted armies that had been fighting defensive actions for months in Poland along the Vistula. What was left of these forces were supposed to hold the Oder front and fight to the death. By this period of the war the Polizei Division was assigned to the 11th SS Panzer Army in what was known as Operation Solstice. Surviving elements of the division fought a number of heavy battles including a counter-attack at Arnswalde.

Two photographs taken in sequence showing a ceremonial parade. Following bitter action in Operation Solstice, what was left of the Polizei Division withdrew and moved east of the Oder. In March 1945 the 11th SS Panzer Army was reorganized and assigned to operations on the Western Front. This also comprised the bulk of the Polizei Division which moved with the 11th SS.

Two photographs showing a narrow-gauge railway and a special narrow-gauge train towing men and supplies to the front during fighting in Army Group North during the last months of the war. In one of the photographs a Zeltbahn shelter quarter has been erected on the flatcar.

(**Above**) Also during the last year of the war on the Eastern Front, muddy roads represented a formidable foe. The mud produced from a few hours of rain was enough to turn a typical Russian road into a quagmire. In this photograph a Polizei motorcyclist, crew member and another soldier struggle to get a motorcycle combination through the mud.

(**Opposite, above**) A group of disheveled troops pose for the camera with their amphibious four-wheel-drive Schwimmwagen.

(**Opposite, below**) Polizei troops with full kit and wearing camouflage smocks pose for the camera before being transported to the front in 1945. By this late period of the war the atmosphere among the troops became a mixture of foreboding and despair as the Russians pushed from the east and the Allies advanced from the west. The 11th SS Panzer Army, to which the Polizei had been assigned, had been given the task of launching an offensive designed to dislocate the threatened enemy advance on Berlin, but had been halted against massive attacks. When the final push on Berlin begun on 16 April, the 11th SS Panzer Army retained only three reliable divisions. The Polizei had been badly mauled during heavy fighting around Hela and moved towards Berlin to support dwindling forces. Fighting alongside units of the Polizei was 18th Panzergrenadier-Division, 11th SS Panzergrenadier-Division 'Nordland' and SS Brigade 'Nederland', which had been sent out of the capital to help stem the Russian advance. Inside the ruined city, part of the 15 Waffengrenadier-Division der SS from Latvia was ordered to take up defensive positions together with the Belgian 'Langemarck' and 'Wallonien' Divisions and the remaining volunteers of the French 'Charlemagne' Division. All of these Waffen-SS troops were to take part in the last, apocalyptic struggle to save the Reich's capital from the clutches of the Red Army.

(**Opposite, above**) A signalman on a field telephone. A signals battalion provided field telephone and radio communications support within a German division, and linked all subordinate units. Telephone and radio troops had switchboards, laid wires and cables for telephone communications and connected with corps headquarters.

(**Above**) The crew of a 7.5cm PaK 40 in a defensive position in the Baltic theatre. Although thinly scattered during the last battles in Eastern Europe, this anti-tank gun proved its worth on the Eastern Front and was capable of disabling heavy Soviet tanks. Waffen-SS gunners in particular were able to demonstrat the efficacy of the weapon in action in a number of armoured assaults.

(**Opposite, below**) An interesting photograph showing Polizei troops standing beside a muddy road next to a column of support vehicles. In front of them is a line of StuG.IVs which is led by what appears to be a rarely photographed Befehlspanzer IV.

Polizei medics aid one of the many soldiers injured during the last months of the war.

Organizational History

Division Composition

1939 Police Regiments 1, 2 and 3
      Artillery Regiment 500 (Heer)

1943 SS-Panzergrenadier Regiment (Polizei-Division) 1, 2 and 3
      Wirtschafts Battalion 300 (Heer)
      Nachschub Dienste 300 (Heer)

1944 SS-Panzergrenadier Regiments 7 and 8
      SS-Artillerie Regiment 4
      SS-Sturmgeschütz Abteilung 4
      SS-Feldersatz Bataillon 4
      SS-Feldgendarmerie Truppe 4
      SS-Kriegsberichter-Zug 4
      SS-Polizei-Veterinär Kompanie 4
      SS-Sanitäts Abteilung 4
      SS-Wirtschafts Battalion 4
      SS-Panzer Instandsetzungs Abteilung 4
      SS-Dina 4
      SS-Pionier Battalion 4
      SS-Panzer-Aufklärungs-Abteilung 4
      SS-Nachrichten-Abteilung 4
      SS-Flak Abteilung 4
      SS-Panzerjäger Abteilung 4
      SS-Panzer Abteilung 4
      Stab der Division

Armee of East Prussia – April 1945 (Formerly Second Army)

Reserves
Infantry-Divisions 102, 61, 69, 367, 7, 203 and 83
10 Jäger-Brigade
Volksgrenadier-Divisions 349, 548 and 31
'Hela'
4 SS-Panzergrenadier-Division 'Polizei'

Evacuated and destroyed units (January–April 1945)

56 and 131 Infantry-Divisions (Destroyed in the Heiligenbeil cauldron in March 1945. Remnants escaped to Pomerania.)

102 Infantry-Division (Destroyed in the Heiligenbeil cauldron in March 1945. Remnants were absorbed by the 28 Jäger-Division. Some units managed to retreat to Western Pomerania where they formed Division-Gruppe 102.)

215 Infantry-Division (General Bruno Frankewitz. The division was destroyed in battles on the Tucheler Heide and Gotenhafen in March 1945. Remnants were absorbed into 32 Infantry-Division in early April 1945.)

251 Infantry-Division (Disbanded in March 1945. The staff was transferred to Swinemünde.)

286 Infantry-Division (Destroyed at Neukuhren in the Samland in April 1945. Remnants integrated in 95 Infantry-Division. Staff evacuated to Swinemünde.)

292 Infantry-Division (Destroyed in the Heiligenbeil cauldron in March 1945. Remnants were integrated into 170 Infantry-Division.)

337 Volksgrenadier-Division (Destroyed at Danzig. Remnants were integrated into 391 Defence-Division. On 11 April 1945 it was destroyed in the Halbe pocket.)

349 Volksgrenadier-Division (Destroyed in the Heiligenbeil cauldron in March 1945. Remnants were integrated into 21 Infantry-Division in April.)

389 Infantry-Division (Defensive actions in Danzig and West Prussia. Division evacuated to Swinemünde in early April 1945.)

541 Volksgrenadier-Division (Destroyed in Heiligenbeil cauldron in March 1945. Remnants evacuated to Swinemünde.)

547 Volksgrenadier-Division (Destroyed in East Prussia in late January 1945. Remnants integrated into 170 Infantry-Division.)

549 Volksgrenadier-Division (Destroyed in East Prussia in late January 1945. Remnants reformed at Pasewalk in Pomerania.)

562 Volksgrenadier-Division (General Helmuth Hufenbach killed on 27 March 1945. The division was destroyed in the Heiligenbeil cauldron.)

2 Panzergrenadier-Division 'Hermann Göring' (Destroyed in the Heiligenbeil cauldron in March 1945. Remnants evacuated in early April.)

18 Panzergrenadier-Division (Destroyed in the Heiligenbeil cauldron. A new 18 Panzergrenadier-Division was built from elements of the original in late March 1945.)

24 Panzer-Division (General Gustav-Adolf von Nostitz-Wallwitz was badly wounded on 25 March 1945 in the Heiligenbeil cauldron. Division was destroyed.)

4 SS-Panzergrenadier-Division Polizei (Shipped from Hela to Swinemünde in April 1945.)

Ranks

German Army	Waffen-SS	British Army equivalent
Gemeiner, Landser	Schütze	Private
	Oberschütze	
Grenadier	Sturmmann	Lance Corporal
Obergrenadier		
Gefreiter	Rottenführer	Corporal
Obergefreiter	Unterscharführer	
Stabsgefreiter		
Unteroffizier	Scharführer	Sergeant
Unterfeldwebel	Oberscharführer	Colour Sergeant
Feldwebel		
Oberfeldwebel	Hauptscharführer	Sergeant Major
Stabsfeldwebel	Hauptbereitschaftsleiter	
	Sturmscharführer	Warrant Officer
Leutnant	Untersturmführer	Second Lieutenant
Oberleutnant	Obersturmführer	First Lieutenant
Hauptmann	Hauptsturmführer	Captain
Major	Sturmbannführer	Major
Oberstleutnant	Obersturmbannführer	Lieutenant Colonel
Oberst	Standartenführer	Colonel
	Oberführer	
Generalmajor	Brigadeführer	Brigadier General
Generalleutnant	Gruppenführer	Major General
General	Obergruppenführer	Lieutenant General
Generaloberst	Oberstgruppenführer	General
Generalfeldmarschall	Reichsführer-SS	Field Marshal

Notes

Notes

Notes